SOLVE THAT CRIME!

Counterfeit!

Stopping Fakes and Forgeries

Richard Spilsbury

 Enslow Publishers, Inc.
40 Industrial Road
Box 398
Berkeley Heights, NJ 07922
USA
http://www.enslow.com

This edition published in 2009 by Enslow Publishers, Inc.

Library of Congress Cataloging-in-Publication Data

Spilsbury, Richard, 1963-
  Counterfeit! : stopping fakes and forgeries / Richard Spilsbury.
    p. cm. — (Solve that crime!)
  Includes bibliographical references and index.
  Summary: "Learn how forensics solves the mystery of counterfeit and forged objects, from fake money to false Vermeers"—Provided by publisher.
  ISBN-13: 978-0-7660-3378-8
  ISBN-10: 0-7660-3378-3
  1. Forgery. 2. Fraud. I. Title.
  HV6675.S76 2009
  363.25'9668—dc22

                                2008033310

Printed in the United States of America
10 9 8 7 6 5 4 3 2 1

For The Brown Reference Group Ltd.
Project Editor: Sarah Eason
Designer: Paul Myerscough
Picture Researcher: Maria Joannou
Managing Editor: Miranda Smith
Editorial Director: Lindsey Lowe
Production Director: Alastair Gourlay
Children's Publisher: Anne O'Daly

Cover photo: Oleksandr/ Shutterstock

Photo Credits: Alamy Images, pp. 20, 43; Corbis, pp. 13, 26, 33, 35, 42; Dreamstime, p. 9; Fisher Forensic Document Laboratory, Inc., pp. 40–41; Getty Images, pp. 11, 29; iStockphoto, p. 19; PA Photos, p. 27; Photoshot, p. 36; Rex Features, p. 24; Science Photo Library, pp. 4, 31; Shutterstock, pp. 5, 6, 7, 8, 12, 14, 15, 16, 17, 18, 21, 22, 23, 25, 28 (r and l), 30, 32, 37, 38, 39, 40, 44; Wikipedia, p. 10.

Contents

Making fakes

Criminals worldwide create fake objects and sell them to other people. They do this to make money, even though it cheats other people, organizations, and even governments.

What is a counterfeit?

A counterfeit is a copy of something that is made to fool people into thinking it is real. For example, you may go to a store and try to buy something with a $10 bill. It looks like any other $10 bill, but the store will not let you use it because they discover it is a counterfeit. You cannot spend a worthless fake. You have been deceived into thinking it is real. So, you have been cheated out of $10 by the people who made the counterfeit.

4

A forensic scientist examines a forged painting under a light microscope. An expert eye can pick out areas of retouched paint.

Billions of dollars of fake bills are seized every year.

Master copiers

Forgery is the process of making, or changing documents or other objects to be, counterfeits. Forgers are often skilled at copying real objects. For example, an art forger may paint pictures just like those of a famous painter, such as Picasso. Forgery is not illegal in itself. It becomes illegal when someone tries to pretend the fake is the real thing. The art forger who sells their forgery as if it were actually created by Picasso is committing a crime. Crimes that involve deception such as this are known as fraud.

Fighting fraud

The global trade in fake goods is estimated at around six percent of all trade, or hundreds of billions of dollars each year. Many people are trying to stop counterfeit trade. Forensic scientists are trained to spot fakes. They use many different kinds of technology to help them find evidence. This can help the police arrest the counterfeiters. It can also be used by customs officers, who help control the flow of goods between countries.

Money under the spotlight

Every fake banknote (paper money) represents a theft of real money. Police work with forensic teams to find counterfeit money and remove it from circulation. They try to catch those who commit this form of fraud, and then punish them. The job is difficult because worldwide there are tens of millions of dollars worth of fake money mixed in among genuine money. The fake money is constantly exchanged for goods, mostly without the knowledge of the person spending it!

If you suspect that a banknote may be a fake, hand it in to the police.

How professional forgers work

Professional forgers use printing plates to make counterfeit money. A different plate is used for each color on the original bill. The forgers find ink and paper that match those used for originals. It takes great skill to create printing plates. Criminals employ trained print workers in different parts of the world.

Amateur notes

People who are inexperienced in creating fake money are called amateur forgers. They often use color photocopiers, scanners, and computer printers to create fake paper money. This equipment is widely available and easy to use. However, the copies produced are not very accurate and usually do not fool many people.

Real money is printed onto cotton paper, which gives a perfect finish. It is easy to spot money printed onto copier paper—the ink is often blotchy and the images may be blurred.

TRUE CRIME...

Operation Bernhard

During World War II, the Nazi Party developed a plan called Operation Bernhard. The plan was to distribute fake money for use in Britain and the United States. The idea was that, if people spent these counterfeit banknotes, the value of real money would fall, which would weaken the economies of Germany's enemies. The Nazis trained 142 forgers to make millions of United States and British banknotes. By the time they had created perfect forgeries, the war had ended. The Nazis dumped the fake money into a German lake and it was discovered there in the 1950s!

IN THE LAB

The fiber of money

One way that forensic scientists determine if currency is real is by fiber analysis. US banknote paper is made from cloth fibers with man-made fibers mixed in. These give the bills greater strength and flexibility than regular paper fibers. Most countries use cotton paper from one paper factory. Each factory uses fibers that are slightly different. For example, some fibers are fluorescent (they glow in the dark) when viewed in ultraviolet light. Genuine bills from the US Treasury include red and blue cotton fibers. Scientists examine the shape and color of fibers to ensure the money is genuine.

A watermark shows up best when a bill is held up to the light.

Difficult to copy

A dollar bill may not look like anything more than an image printed on a small rectangle of paper. But there is more to it than meets the eye. Government printers who make real bills add many different security features to make it very difficult to copy the bills. These features are easily spotted by experts such as bank workers and forensic scientists. If the security features are missing, or are wrong, the money is fake.

Here are a few of the security features found in banknotes:

Watermarks are a distinctive design created within the paper when it is made, rather than being printed on top of the paper. They are usually invisible but show when you hold the note up to the light.

Holograms are patterns that resemble a three dimensional object, such as a face, when viewed from certain angles. Holograms are usually found in embossed (raised) circles or other shapes that look as if they are made of silver foil.

Printed images have some lines so fine and delicate that it would be impossible for a photocopier or scanner to read them, and so reproduce them. These lines may appear blurred if copied, which shows the bill is a fake.

EXAMINE THE EVIDENCE

Money studies

Can you spot some of the security features on different banknotes? Collect some currency from a few different countries—you could ask your friends or relatives who have traveled. Use a desk lamp and a magnifying glass to examine the bills for fibers, holograms, watermarks, and other features. Which features would be hardest for a counterfeiter to fake?

9

Printing serial numbers that are unique to each note is a method used in European countries to help prevent banknote forgery.

Making safer
bills

Since 1996, the United States Treasury has created new currency with improved security measures to make dollar bills harder to forge. In 2008, the Treasury issued the new $5 bill.

On the surface

Artists prepare the printing plates by cutting the image of the $5 bill into the metal. This process is called engraving. The plate is covered with sticky ink and then rubbed clean, leaving ink only in the grooves. The printing press pushes the plate firmly onto the paper, which pushes the paper down except in the grooves where the ink remains. In this way, the printed lines are raised above the rest of the banknote. A forgery will rarely have raised lines like these.

The new $5 bill has many special security features that are easier for people to check.

Printing the detail

Some of the lines in the image on the $5 bill are incredibly fine (or thin). They are so fine that a photocopier or scanner will not recognize them as separate lines, so they will come out blurred if copied. In fact, some of the lines are strings of tiny words that can only be seen through a strong magnifying glass. For example, "USA FIVE" is printed on the lower "5" of the $5 bill.

Spot the color!

The $5 bill is printed with a special ink that can change color from green to black. It can do this because tiny metal flakes are added to the ink. The flakes reflect light differently depending on the angle you look at the bill from, creating the different colors. Only the US Treasury are able to buy the materials that make up this ink.

Using the thread

New $5 bills have security threads made of thin foil, or plastic strips, embedded in the paper. Genuine threads glow blue under ultraviolet light. The thread is in different places on bills of different values, so forgers cannot remove the "5" thread from a $5 bill and replace it with a "20" thread. Even if the new lettering looks genuine, the position of the thread shows that the note is a counterfeit.

11

Officials from the Federal Reserve Bank announce the launch of the new $5 bill in Washington, DC in 2008.

Copying coins

A round the world, billions of coins are in use every day. There are also thousands of old coins that are no longer used for payment, that are traded and collected by enthusiasts. Many of these coins—both old and new—are fakes.

Making fakes

Forging coins is not a new idea. The earliest coins were made from precious metals such as gold and silver. Forgers created fake coins by coating cheaper metals with a thin layer of the precious metal, or by mixing other metals to look like the metal. Today's forgers often copy images and words stamped onto real coins to make molds. They then pour molten (melted) metal into the molds to make casts of the originals.

Unlike bills, many people do not bother to check change given in coins. Making counterfeit coins can be very profitable for criminals.

IN DEPTH

Metal matters

Different types of coins are made from different metals. For example, the penny is 97.5 percent zinc coated with 2.5 percent copper. The quarter is coated with 8.33 percent nickel and is 91.67 percent copper. The blend of metals that is used in each type of coin gives it a particular color. Each type of coin also has a particular size and weight of metal. For example, a quarter weighs 5.67 grams and a dime weighs 2.268 grams.

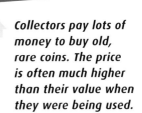

Collectors pay lots of money to buy old, rare coins. The price is often much higher than their value when they were being used.

Spotting fakes

Fake coins are fairly easy to spot. Casts are obvious because tiny air bubbles and cracks form when the molten metal cools. Fakes that are stamped onto metal often have a less detailed image that is also not centered on the coin. Reeds are the narrow bars around the edge of a coin. Each type of coin has a particular number of reeds. For example, a quarter has 119 evenly spaced reeds. Reeds are tricky to fake, because the edge of a coin is so narrow.

Electronic coin testers

Modern ticket and vending machines can identify fake coins automatically! When you put a coin in the slot, it passes through an electric field. Only coins made of the right-sized piece of the correct metal conduct the right amount of electricity. In a second test, coins are made to roll past a magnet. The magnet attracts the metal and slows down the rolling coin. Sensors detect the change in speed. Each type of coin changes speed by a different amount. Fake coins will usually fail one or both of these tests.

Dangerous counterfeits

Criminals around the world also make and sell counterfeit medicines. According to the World Health Organization (WHO), a tenth of all medicines for sale are counterfeit. Fake medicines can be dangerous because they may make people sicker, or even kill them. They are also not as effective as real medicines, so people do not get better.

Types of fake medicines

Criminals make and sell many different fake medicines to treat all kinds of diseases, from AIDS to malaria. Malaria is one of the world's biggest killer diseases. It is passed on by some types of female mosquitoes when they bite people. Chemicals in real antimalarial drugs, such as artesunate, are used to treat severe malaria after it has developed in a person.

The active ingredient

The chemical that makes a medicine effective is called the "active ingredient." Fake drugs contain

◄ *A forensic chemist uses a microscope to examine traces of chemicals taken from a batch of fake drugs.*

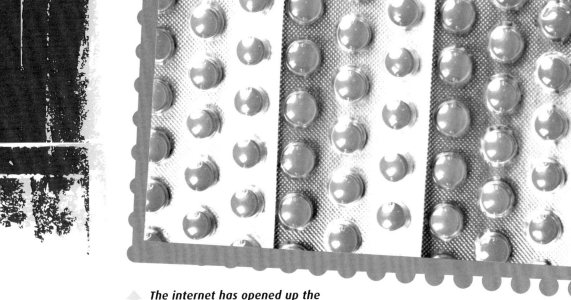

The internet has opened up the market for fake drugs. This makes it hard to track down the people who commit these crimes.

less (or none) of the expensive active ingredients, but the buyer still pays the price of the genuine medicine. Using too little of the active ingredient found in the original drug to treat malaria makes treatment using the fake medicine ineffective.

Finding the fakes

Forensic chemists find out which chemicals are used to make fake drugs. They use a wide range of chemical tests and devices such as spectroscopes to test drugs. These detect and measure how the chemicals in the drugs respond to electricity, heat, or light. The chemists also test the medicines by adding different chemicals that react with the active ingredients. This often creates a change in their color or in their weight.

TRUE CRIME...

Trading fakes

In 2006, Chinese authorities arrested a man in southern China for selling fake antimalarial drugs. Forensic chemists bought the fake artesunate tablets from different chemists across Southeast Asia. After the drugs were analyzed, forensic chemists revealed that 38 percent of the samples had no artesunate in them at all. Most had too little to combat malaria effectively. Scientists identified minute amounts of plant pollen in the tablets as having come from southern China. They then tracked down the factory where the counterfeit tablets were made.

Fake luxuries

Many people like to buy luxury items, such as jewelry, perfumes, and designer clothes and bags. They are prepared to pay a lot more to buy the very best. However, criminals produce cheap copies of luxury brands to fool people into buying them. Forensics experts are vital in the job of spotting the fake goods and in helping law-enforcement officers to catch the forgers.

Making fake perfumes

Genuine perfumes are made by expert perfume blenders. They may mix together hundreds of different scents to create a unique blend. Some forgers try to mimic the original perfume using unusual ingredients. For example, some fake perfumes have been found

Forensic scientists are able to test a perfume to see if the chemicals it is made from match those found in the genuine item.

Laboratory analysis of perfume is time-consuming. A Brazilian scientist has developed a system that can analyze a scent in just two minutes. It is a portable machine that compares the chemical signature of vapor from a real scent with vapor from a fake. The signature shows the proportions of different chemicals used to make the perfume, and should be the same in every bottle of genuine fragrance. Counterfeit versions have different signatures, because forgers are rarely able to match the original exactly.

Street traders often sell big-name brands of watches at bargain prices. These items are most likely fakes.

to contain pond water and even goat's urine! These unpleasant ingredients were chosen to provide musky smells in the counterfeit scent. A bigger problem is when forgers use chemicals that can be harmful to people. Some of the chemicals in fake perfumes give people skin rashes.

Identifying fake perfumes

Some fake perfumes are easy to spot. They may be packed in poorly printed wrapping. They may be sold on the street, rather than in well-known stores. Other fake perfumes are presented quite professionally. To stop the cheats, some perfume companies add packaging tags that contain tiny particles that can be identified under a microscope. However, the only way to identify some fake perfumes is to have their contents analyzed by forensic scientists. One test is to heat up the perfume. Different substances in the liquid evaporate at different temperatures. Scientists condense the vapors (gases) in cooled tubes, then identify the separate liquids.

Gemstones

To make counterfeit jewelry, crooks make fake gemstones that look like the genuine items. They use machines to turn hard plastic or glass into fake diamonds, emeralds, or other gems. They may even create doublets, which are chunks of cheap stone with a thin slice of real gemstone on top. Forensic scientists test the gems in different ways. For example, a genuine diamond cannot be scratched with anything but another diamond or a diamond-coated blade.

18

Garments and bags

Fake clothes, handbags, and shoes are widely available from markets, the internet, and even major stores. They are usually copies of goods made by popular sports brands such as Adidas or Nike, or expensive designer brands such as Chanel or Gucci. Criminals who create these goods rely on the public easily recognizing their brand names, logos, and designs.

Crooks are waiting to make copies of designer clothes almost as soon as the fashion shows are over.

TRUE CRIME...

Shoe scam

In July 2003, police seized 25 truckloads of Nike and Adidas shoe parts from assembly shops in Ho Chi Minh City in Vietnam. Working on a tip-off from Nike, Vietnamese authorities had uncovered a "leakage" scam. Workers in a genuine Nike factory had stolen defective shoe parts. They had sold them to assembly shops, where workers were mending or disguising the defective parts. They were then using the parts to make fake shoes to export to other countries.

⬆ *An expert can tell if a gem is genuine by examining it under a magnifying glass called a loupe.*

Some fake garments are simply mass-produced, poor-quality items with a fake designer label stuck onto them. Others are look-alikes. These are well-made copies of an original that are sold with a different label. For example, some garments feature a check pattern very similar to the characteristic design used on expensive Burberry clothing.

Other fakes are actually originals! Some designer bags sold cheaply on the street are made in the same factories, using the same materials and designs as those sold in expensive stores. Criminals may bribe the factories to let them have the bags cheaply, then sell them at a higher price.

EXAMINE THE EVIDENCE

Beneath the label

Look at some branded goods such as clothes, perfumes, and shoes in your home or at your local market. Can you tell if they are fakes or genuine items? Some tell-tale clues on fake clothes include peel-off brand labels, labels that are spelled incorrectly or having no label showing where the garment was made.

Pirated copies

Counterfeit CDs and DVDs are known as pirated copies. They are widely available on the internet, from mail-order stores, and from street vendors. Many people are happy to pay much less than in stores to see a new movie on a pirated DVD or hear the latest tracks on a fake CD. This is illegal. Criminals around the world earn at least $4.6 billion from music piracy each year.

Pirated CDs are much cheaper than the original CDs, but the quality of the recording is often terrible.

Piracy problems

When people buy an album or movie, part of the money goes to the creator as a royalty. Pirated copies generate no royalties, and fewer copies of the genuine discs are sold. Shops get less money, too. Pirated computer software causes companies and stores to lose around $11–12 billion each year. China and Vietnam are hotspots for the production of pirated discs.

Getting the data

Criminals get the data for pirated DVDs from several different kinds of sources. They may get copies of originals from people who work in film studios or software houses. They may download files from file-sharing sites on the internet. They may also make illegal recordings of original works. Some pirated DVDs are created by recording on a camcorder in a movie theater!

Finding fault

Most pirated copies are easy to spot. The cover may be poorly printed or have spelling mistakes. The quality may also be poor, with blurred images and poor sound, sometimes in the wrong language. Recording companies often try to stop criminals by putting coded information on DVDs to prevent them from being copied.

TRUE CRIME...

Early Windows

In February 2002, 28-year-old John Sankus Jr. of Philadelphia was sentenced to 46 months in prison for leading an international piracy ring called DrinkorDie. This group of about 60 people from the US, Australia, Norway, and other countries illegally copied and distributed computer software. Computers belonging to some DrinkorDie members contained enough hacked software to fill 700,000 discs.

21

Criminals burn genuine software onto blank discs and sell the pirated copies for huge profits.

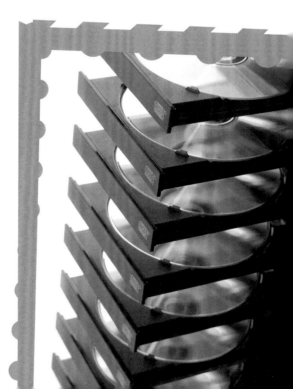

Suspicious spares

Many machines have parts that can be replaced when they wear out. Spare parts include batteries, lightbulbs, memory cards, tires, and windshields. Criminals make cheap copies of genuine spares, because the global trade in fake spares is big business. Automobile manufacturers estimate that the loss of sales in genuine spare parts costs them around $12 billion each year. This is enough money for the industry to employ an extra 200,000 workers!

Fitting cars with counterfeit parts is very dangerous— the parts could fail and cause the car to crash.

Spare appeal

Spares are always in demand, because parts wear out or fail. When companies need a spare part, they may not have time to shop around. When a truck is not in use because it is waiting for new tires, for example, a transportation company cannot carry as many goods and so loses money. Fake spares that look like the real thing are cheap to make, so consumers are attracted by parts that are cheaper than usual.

Dangerous batteries

Batteries are made of chemicals that react to produce electricity. Forgers sometimes use the wrong chemicals when they make batteries. The reaction between these chemicals makes electricity, but it can also produce lots of heat. Overheating batteries can affect the parts inside battery-operated devices, from cell phones to MP3 players. Such overheating may cause damage or even make the device explode!

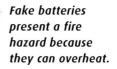

Fake batteries present a fire hazard because they can overheat.

23

Dangerous fakes

Fakes may look like the real thing, but they do not always work properly and can be dangerous. Sometimes you can spot a fake by the differences in the packaging. Fake items often become obvious only after things have gone wrong. In one example, forensic investigators realized fires under cars were being caused by a fake brand of brake pad. Real brake pads are normally coated with metal filings that rub against discs inside the wheels to slow cars. The pads on the investigated cars were fakes. They were coated with sawdust and grass, then sprayed to look like metal. The heat caused by braking set the pads on fire and caused the drivers to crash.

TRUE CRIME...

Fakes in the sky!

In the late 1970s, fake airplane parts were discovered that could have cost lives. The parts were pumps used to fold the landing wheels in and out of Boeing 727 and 737 airplane wings. The counterfeit pumps were made from a chrome-covered steel rather than from solid chrome. Solid chrome does not rust, but steel does. If the fake spares had been used, the chrome would have chipped off and the metal below would have rusted. Without pumps to operate the landing wheels, the airplanes probably would have crashed.

Looking closely at art

The most valuable works of art by the best artists sell for millions of dollars. With so much money at stake, criminals commission talented artists to fake copies of paintings, drawings, and sculptures. If the fakes can fool the experts and sell as the genuine items, the criminals can pocket a lot of money. Art experts and forensic scientists use their knowledge to uncover fakes and help find the criminals responsible.

The auction house Sotheby's offers a Picasso for sale in 2008. Art experts claim that one or two out of every ten works of art sold at auction are fakes.

Forging art

There is a wide range of fake art for sale. Some forgeries are clumsy copies of real art. Other forgeries are good copies of famous artists or periods in art. Forgers use different techniques to make their images look older. For example, they paint on old pieces of canvas, or they age frames by drilling "insect" holes in the wood. Some forgers use chemicals such as acids on the paint to age the paintings.

Finding faults

Art experts often find fakes using their expert knowledge of real artists. Some famous artists have a distinctive style of brushwork. Marks on a sculpture made with modern tools look different from those made with the tools available in the past. Experts also examine the history of paintings. They look at auction house records to track when a work of art has been bought and sold.

Forensic finds

Forensic scientists remove tiny samples of paint, stone, canvas, paper, or other material from a work of art to test it. They analyze

A forensic examiner removes a sample of paint from a work of art. The chemicals in paint have changed over time, so this often reveals a forgery.

25

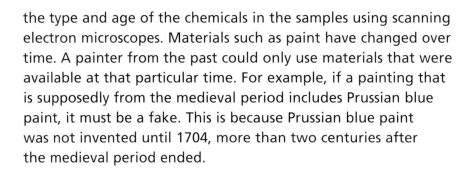

IN DEPTH

Unseen image

To X-ray a painting, a sheet of film is placed behind it. A machine fires X-rays through the canvas. X-rays will move through some paint colors more than through others. An image is created on the film showing the different layers of paint used on the canvas. X-ray images, called radiographs, can also reveal artists' signatures, sketches behind the painting, and even fingerprints.

Laboratories in the ➡ *world's major art galleries use X-ray analysis to ensure that every work of art in their collection is genuine.*

the type and age of the chemicals in the samples using scanning electron microscopes. Materials such as paint have changed over time. A painter from the past could only use materials that were available at that particular time. For example, if a painting that is supposedly from the medieval period includes Prussian blue paint, it must be a fake. This is because Prussian blue paint was not invented until 1704, more than two centuries after the medieval period ended.

Seeing through paintings

Many old paintings were created on previously used canvases or pieces of wood, because these materials were expensive or rare. Sometimes artists painted over other images. Forensic scientists can use X-rays to see these hidden images without damaging the paint. This can help them to figure out if a painting is genuine. For example, a painting was discovered recently that experts believed was painted by Pablo Picasso in the 19th century.

Scientists found that it was painted over another painting in the abstract style. The picture was a fake, because abstract art did not exist until the 20th century.

Confusing the experts

Identifying a work of art as a fake is hard. For example, the French artist Jean Corot and the American artist Andy Warhol signed copies of their works that were actually made by other people they hired to work for them. Also, over time paintings become damaged or dirty. Restorers may clean them up, and even add or remove details. Forensic scientists may then conclude that some materials are fake while others are original within the same work of art. Some "fakes" are later proven to be genuine, using newer art analysis techniques.

Shaun Greenhalgh (left) fooled the art world for many years, with the help of his parents, George (center) and Olive (right).

TRUE CRIME...

Fake family

In 1997, The Art Institute of Chicago bought a small sculpture for $125,000. Experts said it was made by the famous French artist Paul Gauguin. It was later proven to be an expert forgery. It was one of many counterfeit works of art made by a family of three forgers. The Greenhalgh family from Bolton in the United Kingdom made over $1.74 million by selling fake works of art to museums and art galleries around the world. They were finally caught when a museum worker noticed a spelling mistake in an "ancient" stone tablet and realized it was a fake. Forensic workers eventually traced the tablet back to the Greenhalghs. Shaun Greenhalgh was found guilty of fraud and jailed in 2006.

27

Foiling a forger

an van Meegeren from the Netherlands was one of the most famous art forgers of all time. He created paintings in the style of the 17th-century Dutch master, Johannes Vermeer. Van Meegeren sold his fake Vermeers in the middle of the 20th century. He pretended that the paintings were newly discovered originals. Many experts were fooled, because van Meegeren was very good at painting and at making his counterfeits look old.

Although not an exact copy, Van Meegeren's painting (below) copied the style of Vermeer's original (left).

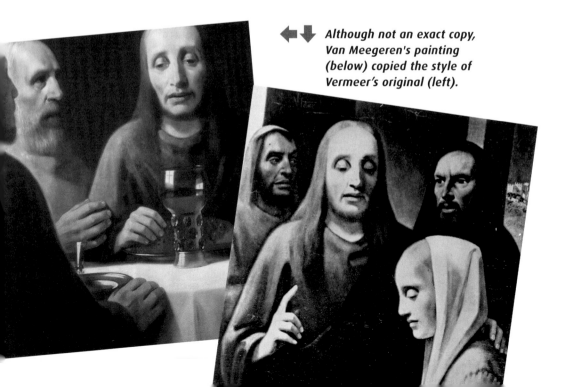

Expert faker

Here are some of the steps Van Meegeren used to create his fakes.

Canvas

He bought genuine 17th-century paintings that he then cleaned with a pumice stone and water.

Paint and brushes

He mixed up his own paints from raw materials that would have been available in the 17th century. He painted using brushes made of badger hair, similar to those used by Vermeer.

Cracking

Once he had painted the canvases, he used a chemical to dry the paint and baked them to make them dry harder. Finally, he rolled up the canvas to crack the paint.

Study

Van Meegeren knew that historians thought Vermeer had traveled to Italy to study the art there. So he painted pictures with themes based on those of 17th-century Italian artists such as Caravaggio.

The mistake

Art dealers became suspicious about the new Vermeers, because it was unusual for so many works by an old master to turn up so quickly. Forensic teams soon found a mistake in a fake called *The Last Supper*. Radiographs showed a hunting scene under the image. Hunting scenes were never painted by Vermeer. Van Meegeren had failed to remove the previous painting from his old canvas.

Revising history

Historical artifacts can also be forged. These include printed materials such as old books, maps, and pieces of music. Since the medieval period, many fake religious relics have been identified. Many of these objects would be of great interest and value if they were genuine, so forensic scientists use various techniques to discover whether they are fakes.

⬇ *Konrad Kujau (below) and the journalist who helped him sell the "Hitler diaries" were put in prison after forensics proved that the diaries were fake.*

Hitler's diaries

One of the most famous forgeries in history was the case of the forged diaries of Adolf Hitler, the Nazi leader of Germany during World War II. In 1981, a German newspaper spent $2 million on what it believed to be Hitler's personal diaries. In 1983, West German police checked the diaries using forensic analysis. Studies of the paper used in the diaries revealed a chemical and fibers that were only used years after Hitler's time. Chromatography identified four different kinds of ink that were not available when Hitler was alive. Closer analysis of the ink suggested the diary was only a few years old!

Police use chromatography to help them solve forgery cases and other instances where people forge signatures.

31

Pen and ink

Chromatography is a test used to separate chemicals. Ink consists of many pigments (chemical colors). To separate the different pigments, ink is first soaked out of the paper and then put into a solvent. Ingredients other than pigments can be seen with ultraviolet or infrared light. Forensic scientists use these findings to figure out the type of pen used, or the date when something was written.

EXAMINE THE EVIDENCE

Chromatography

Draw Xs across the middle of a paper towel with colored washable pens. Hang over a dish of water, so the towel end touches the water. As the water soaks upward, the inks travel with it. Halos of color gather around the Xs. Some color pigment molecules travel further than others. That is why some halos stayed the inital color and others changed color.

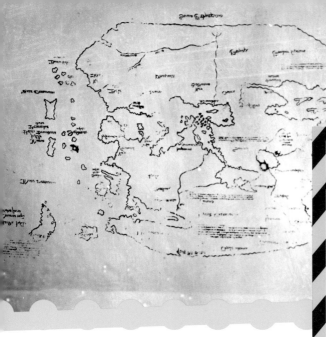

↑ *The Vinland Map is an important find. It suggests that North America was discovered more than 50 years before Columbus discovered the New World in 1492.*

Map forgeries

Map specialists use their knowledge to figure out if an old map is genuine or fake. Early maps were printed by hand, one at a time, by inking an engraved copper plate or woodblock. They were colored by hand, too, so the brushstrokes are visible. An easy way to spot a fake old color map is with a simple magnifying glass.

Pigments on early maps also differ. For example, maps made in medieval times were colored using iron-based inks. These tend to break down over time, leaving yellow or brown stains. Green colors were often made using copper, which can corrode, damaging the paper.

TRUE CRIME...

The Vinland Map mystery

The Vinland Map, discovered in 1957, is dated 1440. It could be the oldest map of North America ever found. Experts disagree about whether or not the map is genuine, however, and they have used different methods to date it. One study looked at the inks used and found traces of titanium dioxide, a pigment that was not used in inks until after the 1920s. This suggested that the map is a modern fake. In 2002, a carbon-dating study of the parchment proved that the paper on which the map is drawn dates from the 15th century. In this case, though, carbon dating cannot be considered conclusive, because the map could have been drawn onto the paper at a later date.

Carbon dating

Carbon dating is a method of establishing exactly how old something is— or rather how long ago it died. Carbon dating (see box at right) only works on things that were once alive, such as plants and animals, because they contain a certain form of carbon called carbon-14. Substances such as metal cannot be carbon dated. Carbon dating can be used to date maps made on paper, because paper comes from wood that was once a living tree.

IN DEPTH

How carbon dating works

A tiny percentage of the total carbon in any living thing is a form called carbon-14, or C-14. Scientists know that when a living thing dies, the C-14 in its body gradually starts to disappear. In fact, it takes 5,568 years for the amount of C-14 to be reduced by one half. By measuring the amount of C-14 in the paper of an old map and comparing it with the percentage that would originally have been there, scientists can accurately date the paper.

33

A forensic scientist studies a map to see if it is a fake.

Investigating the Shroud of Turin

Some Christians believe that the Shroud of Turin is the cloth in which Jesus Christ was wrapped and buried in after he died. It shows a faint imprint of a crucified man, which some believe is an image of Christ. The image could have been made in various ways. Perhaps it is the remains of a painting, or blood and sweat that has somehow imprinted on the cloth. One test of whether or not the Shroud of Turin is a fake is how old it is. Can scientists prove it is really more than 2,000 years old?

1. In 1988, three university laboratories did carbon dating tests on pieces from one small corner of the shroud. All agreed that the fabric dated from between 1260 and 1390 A.D., which is more than 1,000 years after Jesus lived.

2. In 1993, scientist Stephen Mattingly of the University of Texas Health Science Center suggested that the 1988 carbon dating results were wrong, because the pieces tested were contaminated with bacteria. People who handled the cloth could have left bacteria on it. He proposed that this increased the amount of C-14 and made the fabric appear younger than it really was.

3. The 1988 carbon dating results were further discredited by Russian scientist Dmitri Kouznetsov and a Canadian-American physicist named John Jackson. They suggested that the shroud's carbon content changed when it was exposed to a fire in 1532. Smoke from the fire contaminated the cloth with the gas carbon monoxide.

4. In 2005, U.S. chemist Raymond Rogers claimed that the bits of material which were carbon dated were not originally from the shroud. He suggested that they were from different fabric that was used to repair the shroud in medieval times.

5. In 2008, Professor Christopher Ramsey from Oxford University in England, tested some linen samples from the shroud and confirmed smoke contamination. Further tests in the future may finally solve the mystery of the shroud.

35

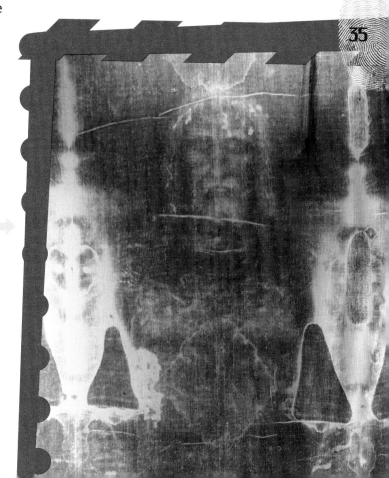

The shroud was found in France in the 14th century. Since 1578, it has been stored safely in a cathedral in Turin, Italy. It is rarely put on public display, because exposing it to light would make it decay more rapidly.

Identity crimes

ost people have to prove their identity at one time or another. They show a passport when they travel. They sign credit card vouchers or type in a password to use a debit card. They do all this to confirm their identity. Criminals forge identity documents for many reasons. They may do it to try to steal money or property, or to escape arrest or travel where they should not. Credit card fraud, including using fake credit cards, cost banks more than $3 billion worldwide in 2007.

Types of identity crimes

Criminals fake identities in many ways. Bank fraud involves getting money from banks by impersonating someone else. The criminal supplies the name, birth date, social security number, or other information that the bank needs to confirm the identity of the

This girl's fingerprints are unique, so a scanner can be used to confirm her identity. A computer compares the scan to records held on a database.

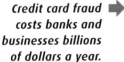
Credit card fraud costs banks and businesses billions of dollars a year.

person who owns the account. Criminals may copy the account holder's signature and pretend to be them when signing documents. They may use stolen or fake bank cards, credit card numbers, or the authorization codes to take money from cash-withdrawal machines.

Stolen identity

Another type of identity crime is called criminal identity theft. Criminals can obtain the official identification documents that "prove" they are someone else. The criminal gives the documents to the police if they are arrested for a crime. When the papers are checked by the police, it may appear that the victim of identity theft is the suspected criminal. If so, the real criminal may be released!

TRUE CRIME...

Identity theft

Michelle Brown got a call in 1998 asking about payment for a new truck. She had no idea about the purchase, so she stopped all her credit cards and notified the bank. However, the criminal continued to use Michelle's identity. Over the next year and a half the criminal spent more than $50,000 on goods and services—and even to buy drugs. Michelle spent more than 500 hours trying to prove she did not spend the money. Eventually the criminal was arrested, but even then the problems were not over. Michelle actually gained a criminal record for a while because the identity thief was booked into Chicago Federal Prison in her name!

Criminals may ➡ replace genuine photos in passports with those of the people who buy the fake documents from the criminals.

Stealing information

There are many ways in which criminals find information to be forged, such as signatures. They may overhear people using identifying information. They may find addresses, bank account numbers, and other personal information by looking through documents, or even old computers, thrown out in the trash—this is called "Dumpster diving." They may steal mail, or break into houses and cars to get information. They may even make completely counterfeit objects, from credit cards to passports, using stolen information.

Cybercrime

One of the fastest-growing crimes today is cybercrime. These crimes involve computers or the internet to steal information and commit fraud. Criminals increasingly find out about their victims using computers. They sometimes search the internet for online government records or browse social-networking sites such as MySpace or Facebook.

Expert computer users can break into computer databases to steal information. This is called hacking. They may even send emails to their victims, pretending to be a trustworthy company or organization. They request information on behalf of the company. This is called phishing.

Forensic techniques

Different people write in different ways. Some people press harder on the paper than others when they write. This leaves tiny impressions, or grooves, in the paper and breaks the paper fibers. Sometimes forgers lean on other documents while they copy, and this may leave impressions of their writing.

Forensic scientists look for these impressions on suspicious documents. They shine a light on the paper from an angle and view the shadows around the impressions using a stereomicroscope. This is like a very powerful magnifying glass that is used with both eyes. When the impressions are too shallow to see clearly, forensic scientists use a machine called an ESDA to look at the documents in more detail.

Even if forgers can copy a signature well, they may not fool the scientists. ➡

IN DEPTH

First impressions

ESDA stands for Electro Static Detection Apparatus. The scientist places a sheet of paper on the machine. The machine attaches a thin plastic film onto the paper. The film has an electrostatic charge, like the charge produced by rubbing a balloon on a sweater and then sticking it to a wall. The charge varies over the film, depending on the depth of the impressions left by the writing marks. Black ink powder sticks to the film to reveal the impressions clearly.

39

> Scanning...
.
0101101110001011001001101
1011010101001101110011110 1
10100111011100101010011010
.
> Identity matched
> Access granted

A biometric scanner analyzes the iris pattern of a woman's eye to confirm her identity.

Identifying ink and paper

Sometimes fraudsters alter the amount of money written on a check, for example from $5 to $500, to get more money than was originally intended by the person who wrote the check. Forensic scientists can spot the differences in ink used on forged documents like this. They use a Video Spectral Comparator (VSC). This machine shines different types of light onto documents, including infrared and ultraviolet light that our eyes cannot see. Ink from different sources may glow or show up differently in these lights. A video camera in the VSC detects the light reflecting from the ink, and displays differences in the inks on a computer screen.

TRUE CRIME...

Famous forger

The most famous identity forger ever was Frank Abagnale from the United States. During the 1960s, he faked documents so he could work as a pilot, lawyer, doctor, and in other careers for which he had no training. He also forged checks and cashed them in different countries. He made more than $2.1 million from his crimes, but he was eventually caught and imprisoned in 1971. In 1974, Abagnale was released early so he could help the US government catch other identity thieves. He now helps banks, companies, and the FBI stop fraud and identity theft. His life story was made into the movie *Catch Me If You Can* (2002), starring Leonardo DiCaprio.

The VSC is also used by scientists to identify differences in paper. Chemicals in paper from different sources will glow differently. Although the paper may look identical at first glance, the equipment will reveal if it comes from a different source. For example, a scientist can use a VSC to spot a fake extra page added to a will. Such evidence may help prove that a criminal has committed fraud or identity theft.

Foiling identity forgers

Security workers have developed ways for people to identify themselves without using signatures. These methods are more difficult for criminals to forge. Smart cards have small computer chips built into them. The chips contain data about an individual, such as a date of birth. Some systems use biometric scanners that are able to view unique patterns in certain parts of the body, such as a fingerprint or the iris in the eye. If patterns are stored in a database, identity can be proven when there is a match.

41

A Video Spectral Comparator (VSC) can show differences in inks and papers, which would reveal faked documents.

Writing identity

Many people have similar handwriting. A person's handwriting may look like that of his or her parents, or resemble the handwriting of other people who learned to write in the same school. Yet each person's handwriting is unique. Subtle differences in the size, shape, and flow of letters make it distinct.

Solving identity crimes

Forensic document examiners help identify criminals by spotting attempts to forge or change writing. These experts look at the shape and slant of words and letters and the neatness of the writing. Document examiners look at how hard the person was pressing when writing. They see if the letters were written carefully, or scrawled in a hurry. They look for repeated words or ways of putting together sentences. The way we write is often similar to how we speak. Someone who makes a lot of grammar mistakes when they talk will probably write that way, too.

When the baby of the famous aviator Charles Lindbergh was kidnapped in 1932, investigators matched the handwriting in this ransom note to that of the suspect to solve the case.

Building a character portrait

Graphologists make hundreds of measurements and evaluations of a sample of handwriting to create a character profile.
For example:
- heavy writing—the person may be under stress
- very small writing—may lack social confidence
- tall letters—may be ambitious
- long bar on small "t"—lively and energetic
- u-shaped bar on small "t"— may be untrustworthy, evasive.

Handwriting analysis can reveal a lot about a person's character.

43

The other side of handwriting

Some people claim that our handwriting can reveal something about the kind of person we are. People with expertise in determining the character of an individual from their writing are called graphologists. Graphologists may examine writing using the same tools as forensic document examiners, such as ESDA. They then create a character portrait, which is a summary of what the writing tells them about the person who wrote the letter. Police officers may then compare the character portrait with what they know about possible suspects. If there is a possible character match, they will investigate the suspect further.

However, many experts are sceptical about the conclusions made by graphologists. They believe that handwriting in an individual can change due to many factors, such as aging or feeling ill. They say that graphology is completely subjective. This means that different graphologists may come up with very different interpretations of the same piece of writing.

Careers in forensics

Do you like searching for clues and solving mysteries? Do you enjoy carrying out scientific experiments for hours at a time? Are you interested in how people catch criminals? If your answers to these questions are yes, then you will probably enjoy a career in forensics.

44

The right skills

People need the right skills to work in forensics. The most useful subjects to study at school are sciences such as chemistry and biology. At college people may take forensics courses. A degree in forensics will include science, but it may also include courses on law and crime. Forensic scientists also need other important skills, such as good communication abilities and attention to detail, because they will typically work on several different cases at the same time.

Some careers in forensic science involve laboratory work, so a background in science is essential.

Laboratory work

Many forensic scientists start work as technicians in forensic laboratories. They apprentice with senior forensic chemists while they develop expertise. Common duties include setting up, operating, and maintaining laboratory instruments and equipment. They monitor experiments, make observations, and calculate and record results. Typical work may involve analyzing anything from fake coins and medicines to paints and perfumes. This analytical background builds important skills for the future. As one forensic scientist says, "It's very hard to get any kind of science work without lab experience, so getting work experience is important."

SALARY CHART

This chart shows what some forensic scientists working in the field of counterfeit and forgery can expect to earn.

Forensic scientist	Approximate salary
Chemist	$46,387—$75,431
Laboratory technician	$46,387—$75,431
Fraud investigator	$46,387—$75,431

45

Fraud experts

Many areas of forensics require fraud specialists, forensic scientists who are experts in finding evidence of forgery, counterfeiting, and other forms of fraud. They may work directly for the police, or for government agencies such as the Secret Service or the FBI. Some work in art galleries or history museums. Other fraud specialists, such as forensic document examiners, may work in banks, accounting firms, or law offices. They may then use lab technicians to help prove that fraud has taken place. Organizations working to stop this kind of crime need receptionists, administrative assistants, and other kinds of support staff. Many career opportunities exist for someone interested in forensics.

Glossary

auction—Sale of something to the person who offers the most money.

carbon dating—When scientists test how much carbon something has to find out how old it is.

carbon monoxide—Invisible, odorless, and poisonous gas produced by burning wood and other fuels.

computer chips—Silicon chips with tiny electronic circuits etched onto them.

condense—Change state from gas to liquid, usually by cooling.

contaminated—Made impure or unsafe by contact with other substances.

data—Any piece of information.

database—Collection of information, usually stored on a computer.

embossed—Decorated with a raised pattern.

evaporate—Change state from liquid to gas, usually by heating.

export—Selling or transferring goods or services to another country.

fluorescent—Glowing by absorbing energy and giving out light.

forensic scientist—Person who uses science and technology to investigate and establish facts in a criminal case.

forgery—Process of making or adapting objects or documents, usually with the intent to deceive others.

fraud—Crime of deliberate deception to steal money, property, or other valuable commodities.

hacking—Breaking into a computer system.

identity theft—Crime of stealing official identification documents to "prove" the criminal is someone else.

infrared—Type of light invisible to our eyes, with wavelengths longer than visible red light.

medieval—Period of history from about 1000 to 1450 A.D.

phishing—Using e-mail or a telephone to persuade a person to give out details about their personal identity

pigments—Substances used to give ink or paint a particular color.

pirated—Illegally copied from an original item for sale and distribution.

pollen—The fertilizing part of flowering plants, consisting of powdery, yellow grains.

printing plates—Surfaces bearing an image for transfer onto paper or other material.

professional—Extremely competent at a profession or job; carrying out an occupation for a livelihood.

relics—Objects from the past with historic value or significance.

royalty—Payment for the right to use someone else's creative work.

shroud—Cloth used to wrap the body of a dead person.

solvent—Liquid used for dissolving another substance to form a solution.

ultraviolet—Type of light invisible to our eyes, with wavelengths shorter than visible violet or blue light.

X-rays—Form of energy that passes through materials to show what is beneath the surface.

Further reading

Books

Cooper, Chris. *Forensic Science*. New York: DK Children, 2008.

Dahl, Michael. *Computer Evidence.* Mankato, Minn.: Edge Books, 2005.

Fridell, Ron. *Forensic Science*. Minneapolis, Minn.: Lerner Publications Co., 2007.

Martin, Michael. *Handwriting Evidence*. Mankato, Minn.: Capstone Press, 2007.

Web sites

There is more information about The Vinland Map, the Hitler Diaries, and many other famous fakes at:

www.pbs.org/wgbh/nova/vinland/fakes.html

To find out more about the technology that helps scientists solve art crime, visit:

http://whyfiles.org/081art_sci/5.html

Find out more about money and counterfeiting at:

www.secretservice.gov/counterfeit.shtml

Index